# HARMONY
## Helps the Hive

Joel & Pippa Pixley

Published by the Co-operative College 2014

www.co-op.ac.uk

Holyoake House, Hanover Street, Manchester M60 0AS

© The Co-operative College

ISBN: 978-0-85195-337-3

Written and illustrated by Joel & Pippa Pixley

Printed by RAPSpiderweb

In the heart of the hive, all hustle and bustle,
Harmony the honey bee **helped herself**
to her favourite snack . . .

. . . but the
honeycomb
was almost
EMPTY!

Harmony and her friends, Hatty and Hazel
wanted to help with the big job of
filling up the honey stores.

They **BUZZED**

with excitement at
the thought of flying far
from home, foraging for food
among the flowers for the first time!

At the door of the hive they met
an old bee called Tatty.

She shared with them
the sweetest nectar . . .

. . . and the most
**magical scent**
they had ever smelled.

Harmony, Hatty and Hazel **ZOOMED** into the sky!

They **zipped** away from the hive and **rollercoaster** raced over the bushes

Harmony **zigged** and **zagged** between the raindrops!

As the cold rain beat down . . .

Harmony shivered beneath a leaf.

I may be feeling sad
and just be a little bee,
but I WON'T GIVE UP
because my hive needs me!

To keep warm she **BUZZED** as fast as she could, and then . . .

. . . the rain stopped,

the sun shone bright,

and that **magical scent** floated all round the tree!

Harmony **hummed** from flower to flower . . .

. . . drinking the yummy nectar and stuffing her baskets with balls of golden pollen.

Harmony headed home

away from the tree

and up, up, up . . .

past the scarecrow

...into the WHOOOSHING WIND!

Carrying her heavy load, Harmony felt she could fly no more.

I may be feeling tired
and just be a little bee,
but I WON'T GIVE UP
because my hive needs me!

She gave one last BUZZ, and then . . .

. . . Harmony could see the beehive just beyond the bushes!

The **breeze** carried her home . . .

... where her friends were waiting!

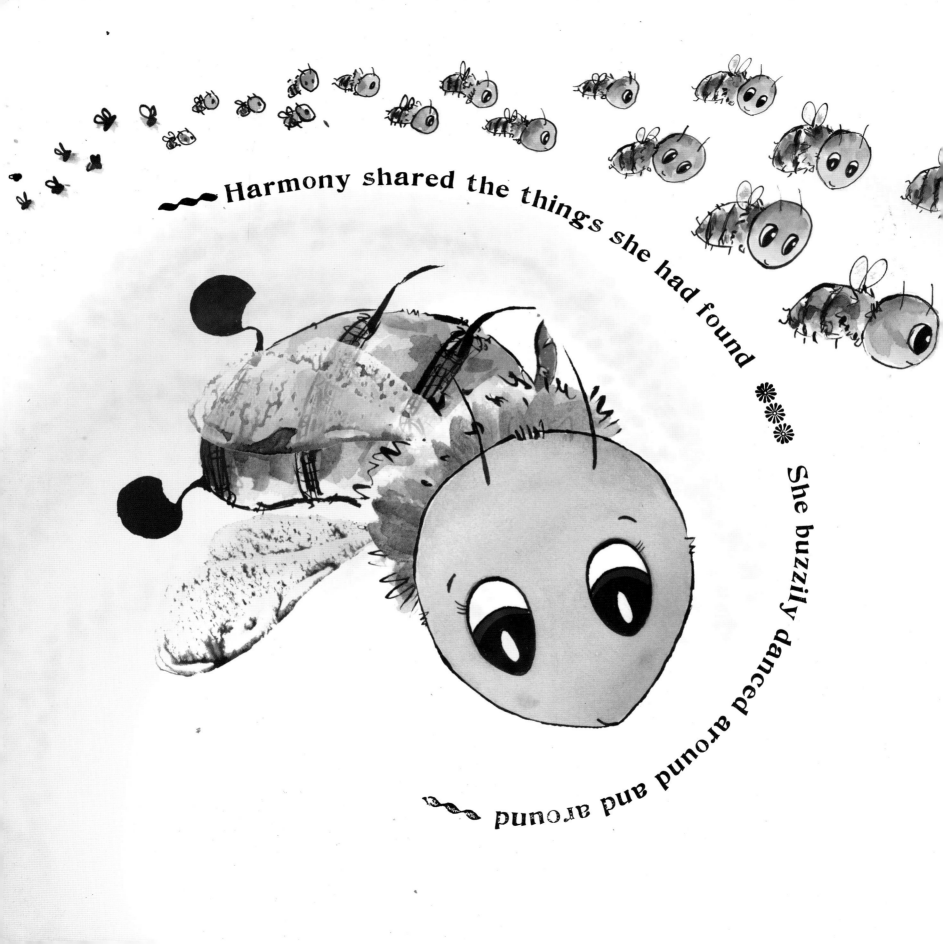

Harmony shared the things she had found ❀❀❀ She buzzily danced around and around and around

Her exciting news spread quickly through the hive.

Hundreds of bees
joined Harmony, Hatty and Hazel
as they set off to gather nectar from the tree.
The hive would soon have plenty of honey stored up!

At the top of the tree, all hustle and bustle,
Harmony enjoyed a sip of sweet nectar . . .

. . . together with all her friends!

Bees are not the only creatures who know how to work together. People are really good at working together, too. When they help each other they can do amazing things!

A long time ago, in the year 1844, a group of people in a town called Rochdale had some very big problems. They didn't have much money and the shopkeepers sold them dirty food which made their children poorly. By working together they set up their own shop where people in the town could buy really good food. It was called a Co-operative Society.

Since then lots of other people have co-operated to start shops, factories, schools, farms, and to build houses to make their lives better.

You can still visit the Rochdale Pioneers' first shop which is now a museum.

Throughout history many co-operatives have used the beehive as a symbol because these tiny insects have so much to teach us about the benefits of working together. Bee images can be found on co-operative buildings, banners, and in books and adverts.

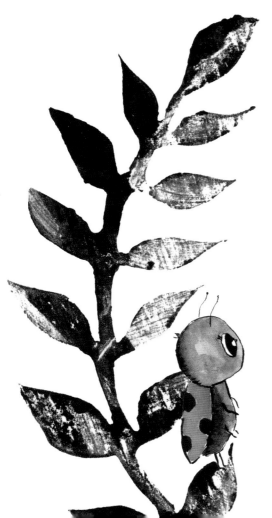

Many plants can only produce fruit thanks to bees delivering pollen from one flower to another.

A honey bee can collect nectar from up to 5000 flowers in one day!

The Co-operative Heritage Trust is a registered charity *(charity number 1121610)* founded in 2007 by the Co-operative Group, Co-operatives UK and the Co-operative College to safeguard the movement's unique and irreplaceable heritage. The Trust's mission is:

*"To inspire people within and beyond the co-operative movement about the origins, development and contemporary relevance of co-operation by collecting, safeguarding and making accessible artefacts and documentation through lifelong learning and research."*

The Co-operative Heritage Trust is custodian of the Rochdale Pioneers Museum (the building where the Pioneers commenced trading on 21 December 1844) and also of the National Co-operative Archive, which holds 200 years of co-operative records. The Co-operative College manages the Museum and Archive on behalf of the Trust.

To find out more about the Rochdale Pioneers go to **www.rochdalepioneersmuseum.coop/** and visit the Co-operative Heritage Trust's website **www.co-operativeheritage.coop/**

The story of Harmony the Honey Bee has been generously supported by:

*Heritage Lottery Fund, Esmée Fairbairn Foundation, John Paul Getty Junior Foundation*

**CO-OPERATIVE
HERITAGE TRUST**